FREEDOM OF INFORMATION ACT 2011

Securing Access to Nigeria Public Record

Temitope Olodo Esq.,

This publication is designed to provide accurate and authoritative information in regard to the subject matter covered. It is sold with the understanding that the publisher is not engaged in rendering legal or other professional service rather than guidance based on personal research and experience.

Copyright ©2015 by Temitope Olodo All rights reserved

Printed in the United States of America

ISBN: **978-1-326-40713-1**

No part of this book may be used or reproduced in any manner whatsoever without written permission except in the case of brief quotations embodied in critical articles and reviews.

For information about the author visit his website:

www.temitopeolodo.com

First Edition

Table of Contents

- Preface
- Introduction to Access to Information
- History of Nigerian FOIA
- How to submit a successful FOI request
- Requests for Information and Penalties
- The Public Interest Test
- The FOIA Exemptions
- FOIA Judicial Decisions outside Nigeria
- Nigeria FOIA Legal Decisions

On the 14th of March 2015, President Muhammad Buhari GCFR delivered a message targeted at the 170 million plus Nigerians both home and abroad entitled "**My 100 Days Covenant with Nigerians**".

In that speech, he made a promise to Nigerians on the issue of access to public record:

"I pledge to... Encourage proactive disclosure of information by government institutions in the spirit of the Freedom of Information Act..."

Many Nigerians are keen for the new president to ensure accessibility to public records and the willingness by Nigerian public institutions to adhere to the provisions of the Freedom of Information Act.

Preface

After a 12 year wait, Nigerian former President Dr. Goodluck Ebele Jonathan signed into law the Freedom of Information (FoI) Bill awaited for by the media community, civil society and information practitioners alike.

The House of Representatives passed the Bill on the 24th of February 2011 and the Senate approved it on March 16, 2011. The harmonised version was passed by both Chambers on 26th of May 2011 and it was conveyed to President Goodluck Jonathan on the 27th of May 2011 for endorsement and he signed it into law on the 28th of May 2011.

The highlight of the Freedom of Information Act 2011 among other things included:

- Section 2(1) of the Act which makes public information and records more freely available.

- Section 3(2) of the Act which provides for public access to public records and information.

President Muhammadu Buhari has promised to improve the FOIA to make it effective.

This book helps to provide further insight into a better implementation of the FOI Act and it is a practical book on FOIA usage.

Introduction to Access to Information

"A popular Government without popular information or the means of acquiring it, is but a Prologue to a Farce or a Tragedy or perhaps both. Knowledge will forever govern ignorance, and a people who mean to be their own Governors, must arm themselves with the power knowledge gives…" -James Madison

The English word for "Information" apparently stems from the Latin word "informare" (to inform) which denotes "to give form to the mind", "to discipline", "instruct", "teach"

The ancient Greek for information is μορφή(*morphe*; cf. morph) and also εἶδος(*eidos*) "kind, idea, shape, set", the latter word was famously used in a technical philosophical sense by Plato (and later Aristotle) to denote the ideal identity or essence of something. "Eidos" can also be associated with thought, proposition or even concept[1]

Therefore, it is safe to state that records are a specialised form of information. Essentially, records are information produced consciously or as by-products of business activities or transactions and retained because of their value. Primarily their value is as evidence of the activities of the organization but they may also be retained for their informational value. Sound records management ensures that the integrity of records are preserved for as long as they are required[2]. A general assessment of all the FOIA legislation across the world reveals that record management maintains a major component of ensuring accessibility.

The international standard on records management, ISO 15489, defines records as "information created, received, and maintained as

---

[1] http://en.wikipedia.org/

[2] Ibid

evidence and information by an organization or person, in pursuance of legal obligations or in the transaction of business".

The International Committee on Archives (ICA) Committee on electronic records defined a record as, "a specific piece of recorded information generated, collected or received in the initiation, conduct or completion of an activity and that comprises sufficient content, context and structure to provide proof or evidence of that activity"[3].

Therefore, record management helps to promote the concept of information accessibility and the Freedom of Information Act is an extension of freedom of speech which is a universal human right recognised under international law.

This means that the protection of freedom of speech as a right includes not only the content, but also the means of expression[4]. Freedom of

---

[3] Ibid

[4] Andrew Puddephatt, Freedom of Expression, The essentials of

information may also denote the right to privacy in the context of the Internet and information technology. As with the right to freedom of expression, the right to privacy is also a recognised human right and freedom of information acts as an extension to this right[5]

Over 85 countries around the world have implemented the FOIA in one form or the other and the first known Act was passed in 1766 by the Swedish and it was known as Freedom of the Press Act

Due to the complexity associated with information held by private companies, most freedom of information laws exclude the private sector from their jurisdiction. Thus, information held by the private sector cannot be accessed as a legal right. However, most FOI Act nowadays allows access to

---

Human Rights, Hodder Arnold, 2005, pg.128

[5]Protecting Free Expression Online with Freenet - Internet Computing, IEEE

information held by private companies that work with public institutions.

Finally, it is important to note that the burden of proof lies with the public institutions to explain why access to information is denied rather with the requester. Therefore, the person making the request for information does not usually have to give an explanation or reason for requesting for information, but if the information is not disclosed a valid reason has to be given by the public body requesting to disclose that information.

History of Nigerian FOIA

The FOI Bill was first introduced into the House of Representatives in 1999 as a private member's Bill on the 8th of December 1999 and published in the federal government's Gazette. Subsequently, the bill went through the first and second reading on the 22nd of February and 13th of March 2000 respectively.

Though, the Bill was passed to the House Committee on Information for further deliberation, the usual public hearing did not hold because the House had already agreed that the Bill was popular. The committee in their plenary session in May 2001 recommended for the Bill to be passed into law but the House was reluctant to pass the Bill and instead it was directed that a public hearing be conducted, which took place on the 3rd and 4th of October 2001 respectively with general supports for the Bill from all the speakers at the public hearing.

For unknown reason, the Bill was never presented to the House after the public hearing until June 2003 after the House was dissolved following the general election in April 2003.

However, the 25th of August 2004 was a unique day in the history of FOI Bill in Nigeria with House of Representatives passing the Bill with the Senate subsequently passed also on the 15th of November 2006.

The significant move by both chambers led to the harmonization of both versions of the Bill by the Conference Committee of the National Assembly on February 14, 2007. The Senate adopted the harmonised version of the Bill on the 21st of February 2007 and House of Representatives did the same on the 27th of February 2007.

Though the Bill was sent to President Olusegun Obasanjo on the 23rd of March 2007[6], he refused to consent to the Bill on the 2nd of May 2007 and instead returned it back to the National Assembly without assent.

After the exit of President Olusegun Obasanjo the process was revamped and fortunately, the House of Representatives passed the Bill on the 24th of February 2011 and the Senate approved it on March 16, 2011.

---

[6] Bill was transmitted to President Olusegun Obasanjo for assent by the National Assembly on March 23, 2007 through his National Assembly Liaison Officer, Senator Florence Ita-Giwa

The harmonised version was passed by both Chambers on 26th of May 2011 and it was conveyed to President Goodluck Jonathan on the 27th of May 2011 for endorsement and he signed it into law on the 28th of May 2011.

The new law signed by Mr. President applies to all arms of government: the Executive, Legislature and Judiciary as well as to all tiers of government: Federal, State, and Local governments including private companies providing services to public sectors.

The enabling of this law has further enhanced Nigeria's compliance with other regional and international obligations that involve ensuring better access to information by Nigerians such as:

- Articles 10 and 13 of the United Nations Convention Against Corruption (2003);

- Article 9 of the African Union Convention on Preventing and Combating Corruption (2003);
- Article 4 of the Declaration of Principles on Freedom of Expression in Africa (2002);
- Article 19 of the UN's International Covenant on Civil and Political Rights (1966);
- The Commonwealth Freedom of Information Principles (1999),
- The UN's Rio Declaration on Environment and Development (1992),
- UN's Principles on Freedom of Information (2000);
- Articles 3 and 4 of the Convention on Access to Information, Public Participation in Decision-Making and
- Access to Justice in Environmental Matters (1998).

How to submit a successful FOI request

Whilst the burden of proof lies with the public institution to provide evidence to explain why information requested for could not be released to a requester (submitter)it is important for a requester to understand how best to approach a request for information and submit a request that would be successful.

That is why it is important that simple but key critical information is not missing in the initial request such as:

1. Name of the requester

2. Full address of the requester

3. Contact telephone/mobile number and email address (where appropriate)

4. Date of sending the letter and signature of the requester

5. Full contact details of the person the information is to be sent to at the public institution

6. Full address of the public institution

Though, it might seem to be basic rules but many requesters forget to include the highlighted information above in their request for public records, therefore making it impossible for the responder (public institution) to provide the information requested for.

Apart from getting the basic information right, it is also important that requesters have a basic understanding of the public institution they are requesting information from, to ensure that they are not requesting for public records that are exempted under the FOI Act or already in the public domain.

In situations where it is impossible to know what information the public institution is holding because they have not complied with section 3 of the FOI Act which requires them to provide a list of all documents that they hold, then there are basic guidelines that the requester needs to adhere to:

- The requester should avoid requesting for records that relate to personal information held

- The requester should avoid requesting for records that are not the primary responsibility of the public institution

- The requester should avoid requesting for records exempted under the law

It is also important that when requesting for information, the requester should ensure that he/she can get proof of postage (recorded delivery) or when the request is delivered by hand, then he/she ensures that someone within the public institution signs to confirm receipt of the request.

When the letter or request for information is submitted and the requester does not get a response or acknowledge within the first four to five days then it is good practice to send a letter of remainder to the public institution.

The process of sending the initial letter and a remainder letter will help the requester when he/she decides to seek legal redress through the High Court which must be done within the first 30 days.

Requests for Information and Penalties

There are procedures and strict rules associated with making request for information under the Freedom of Information Act 2011.

In order for a request for information and application submitted to be successful, there are certain things that need to be done:

- The request must be for an identified record kept by a public institution or private bodies linked to a public institution
- The request should be made in writing though there are exceptions for illiterate or disabled people

- The person making the request should include his/her name and return address
- The person making the request should be prepared to pay for the cost of the photocopying of the information requested for

However, The Act also recognises that there may be valid reasons for withholding information requested for by the requester and that is because the information might be one of the many areas exempted under the law such as:

- Information about investigations and proceedings conducted by public authorities;
- Court records;
- Trade secrets;
- The interests of the United Kingdom abroad;
- The prevention or detection of crime; or
- The activity or interest described in the exemption.
- Information relating to personal information

If a public institution decides to refuse a request for information under the exemption listed above or others, then it is a requirement by law that the public institution inform the requester of the refusal within 7 days of receiving the request under the Freedom of Information Act 2011.

The Act also allows for the public institution to seek for additional time beyond the initial 7 days if for example:

- The information requested could not be reasonably provided within 7 days because of the volume

- The public institution need to consult with other bodies and authorities to enable them provide a detailed information (where information requested cuts across more than one or two public institutions)

Where a public institution refuses to adhere with the provisions of the law on the release of information then the requester of the information could seek legal redress through the High Court on grounds of public interest test.

It is important that when public institutions are refusing a request for information because part of the request falls under an exemption that they are not withholding an entire document. The public institution can still provide a redacted version of the document along with a refusal notice stating why some of the information cannot be released.

Thus, when a public institution decides to refuse a request for information, it is important that they explain which exemption or exemptions they have applied, the reasons for applying them and, where appropriate, fully explain the public interest factors for and against disclosure.

The Public Interest Test

In countries where the FOI law had been enacted, there are certain basic principles that are common trends that cut across the access to information such:

• A common right of access to information held by public authorities.

• The right of access is subject to a range of exemptions and

• Some of the exemptions are subject to a public interest test

Therefore, Nigeria is not alone in the introduction of public interest test in the Freedom of Information Act but what is important, is the understanding of the application of the provisions and its practicability.

Nigeria FOI Act does not define public interest. In some literatures, the public interest test is sometimes referred to as "Public Interest Override" because the public interest consideration sometimes "overrides" the exemption and the section covering 'Landmark FOIA Judicial Decision' provides some insight into the decision of the court on the subject matter.

There is clearly a public interest in access to government information per se. In a well known Australian case the Information Commissioner said:

"It is implicit that citizens in a representative democracy have a right to seek to participate in and influence the processes of government decision making and policy formulation on any issue of concern to them, whether or not they choose to exercise the right. The importance of FoI legislation is that it provides the means for a person to have access to the knowledge and information that will

assist a more meaningful and effective exercise of that right"

Therefore, the "public interest" is a vague concept which is naturally not defined in access to information legislation. This flexibility is intentional because there is an acceptance that public interest will change over time and according to the circumstances of each situation thus, the need that the law does not try to categorically define what is "reasonable."

In a 1995 review of Australian legislation, the Australian Law Reform Commission recognised the difficulties in applying the public interest override but concluded that no attempt should be made to define the public interest in the FoI Act[7].

While Nigeria's experience of freedom of information and legal implications are still young; yet, there are other countries around the world with tested legal principles on public interest test.

---

[7] Information culled from UK Information Commissioner's website

It is important to highlight that when a requester is submitting an application to request information; the requester must test the validity of the request for information. An analysis of public interest cases in the United Kingdom for example reveals the types of considerations that a public institution might take into account in applying the public interest test. The guidance was compiled by the UK Information Commissioner's Office.

Examples of arguments that could weigh in favour of disclosure[8]

- General arguments in favour of promoting transparency, accountability and participation

- Disclosure might enhance the quality of discussions and decision making generally.

---

[8] Culled from UK ICO Website

- The balance might be tipped in favour of disclosure by financial issues. For instance, if the information requested involves a large amount of public money, this might favour disclosure.

- The specific circumstances of the case and the content of the information requested in relation to those circumstances.
- The age of the information might tip the balance in favour of disclosure. The passage of time may impact upon the strength of the public interest arguments.

- The timing of a request, in respect of information relating to an investigation, may be relevant. This would depend on the stage the investigation had reached and how much information was in the public domain.

- The impact (beneficial or otherwise) of disclosure upon individuals and /or the wider public.

Examples of arguments that could weigh in favour of maintenance of the exemption - but only where relevant to the specific exemption being claimed[9]

- The specific circumstances of the case and the content of the information requested in relation to those circumstances.

- The age of the information might tip the balance in favour of maintaining the exemption or exception. The passage of time may impact upon the strength of the public interest arguments.

---

[9] Ibid

- The likelihood and severity of any harm or prejudice that disclosure could cause.

- The significance or sensitivity of the information. For instance, is it "live"?
- The need for a "safe space" for government and civil servants to formulate and debate issues away from public scrutiny.

- The balance might lie in favour of maintaining the exemption or exception in view of the risk of disclosure inhibiting frankness and candour in debate and decision making, especially within government. The strength of this argument depends on clear evidence that it will have this effect.

- In respect of information relating to an investigation, the timing of the request may be relevant, depending on the stage the investigation had reached, and how much information was in the public domain.

- The impact (beneficial or otherwise) of disclosure upon individuals and /or the wider public[10].

The law is clear that a public institution does not have to disclose any information covered by one or more of the exemptions. However, where the public institution is relying on an exemption, then the public interest test must be applied.

In a nutshell, the "public interest" is what serves the interests of the public. Many FOIA exemptions are "qualified", meaning that they are subject to a public interest test.

Even if a qualified exemption or exception is engaged, the information must still be disclosed unless the public interest in maintaining the exemption or exception is greater than the public interest in disclosing it. The decision involves the

---

[10] The public interest test (Version 3) 1 July 2009.

balancing of factors on each side. Under the FOIA, a public institution must apply the public interest separately to each exemption[11].

The public interest must not be used on its own to refuse to disclose information; it must only be used in conjunction with an exemption.

Under the provisions of the law, a public institution is duty bound to respond to a request and communicate information it holds. However, there is no need to comply with that request for information where "the public interest in maintaining the exemption outweighs the public interest in disclosing the information".

Enforcement of the FOI Act currently sits with the Attorney General of the Federation and the Minister is expected to produce an annual report on FOI

---

[11] UK Information Commissioner's Office Guidance. The public interest test Version 3. (13th July 2009)

which must be presented to the two chambers (House of Representatives of Senate).

The FOI Exemptions

The FOI Act also recognises that there may be legitimate reasons for withholding information either for the protection of the public, national security or infringement of individual rights. Thus, the Act sets out a number of categories where exemption rules could be invoked but most of these exemptions are subject to a public interest test.

Some of the exemptions available under the Act include:

- Exemption for international affairs and defence
- Exemption for law enforcement and investigation
- Exemption for personal information
- Exemption for course or research material

It is important to explain that the application of the public interest test would depend largely on whether the identified exemption is either an 'absolute' or 'qualified' exemption.

Specific information deemed to fall under an absolute exemption can be withheld without considering whether there is a public interest in disclosing it especially when it relates to information prohibited from disclosure by other Nigerian legislation such as security matters. For example, if you make a request about where the arrested Boko Haram Sect members are kept and the number of their cell door in the prison or request for information relating to their legal practitioner and client discussion that would amount to breach of confidence; that information would be exempted.

However, if a public institution receives a request for information in which the public authority believes the information could be subjected to public interest test then it is covered by a qualified exemption.

Under the principle of public interest test, a public authority is required to disclose the information unless it considers the public interest in withholding it outweighs that of disclosing it.

Exemption for Commercial interests

The Freedom of Information Act 2011 recognises the need to accord some protection for commercial interest thus the need for some exemptions for information that may affect a business' commercial interest. A commercial interest is anything which affects your business' ability to work competitively.

Therefore, it is advisable that when a public institution receives a request for release of records relating to commercial interest, it is the duty of such public institution to decide whether releasing such information requested would or could harm someone's commercial interests within the provision of the Act. The public institution would then be expected to apply the test of prejudice which will help the public body to decide whether or not a particular disclosure would or could cause prejudice or harm someone's commercial interests. The public institution can seek the views of the business concerned, although the final decision would lay with the public institution.

Trade secrets

If a public institution deems certain information to fall within the remit of trade secret then under the Freedom of Information Act 2011 such information could be exempt from disclosure. However, for any information to be considered to be a trade secret it must have the following components:

- It is used for the purpose of business
- It is not common knowledge
- Disclosing the information would damage the business or give the competitors an advantage

Experience from other countries that have applied FOI laws have revealed that commercial interests will often be paramount even where there is an obvious public interest in the release of the information. The issue in relation to commercial information is often the *timing* of its release.

In an Irish case the Commissioner held that despite the strong public interest, it was premature to release the commercial information concerned, although the authority would be obliged to release it at a later date.

Where the commercial interests of a public agency are concerned, the public interest is more likely to favour release because there is a clear public interest in accountability for public funds.

In one Canadian case, the Commissioner noted that the only fair and reasonable way to balance public interest and corporate loss was to undertake some measure of fact finding with the company concerned.

It is worth stating that in situations involving public safety such as nuclear facilities, the public interest is more likely to be strong enough to override the competitive interests of the third party.

For example in the United States, the Court of Appeal for the District of Columbia Circuit in <u>Public Citizen Health Research Group v. FDA</u>[12], adopted a narrow "common law" definition of the term "trade secret" that differs from the broad definition used in the Restatement of Torts. The D.C. Circuit's decision in <u>Public Citizen</u> represented a distinct departure from what until then had been almost universally accepted by the courts -- that "trade secret" is a broad term extending to virtually any information that provides a competitive advantage.

In <u>Public Citizen</u>, the term "trade secret" was narrowly defined as "a secret, commercially valuable plan, formula, process, or device that is used for the making, preparing, compounding, or processing of trade commodities and that can be

---

[12] 704 F.2d 1280, 1288 (D.C. Cir. 1983)

said to be the end product of either innovation or substantial effort."[13]

The above definition requires that there be a "direct relationship" between the trade secret and the productive process[14].

The United State experience of FOIA application for example reveals that trade secret protection has been recognised for product manufacturing and design information[15], but it has been denied for

---

[13] Ibid

[14] Ibid, accordCtr. for Auto Safety v. Nat'l Highway Traffic Safety Admin., 244 F.3d 144, 150-51 (D.C. Cir. 2001) (reiterating the Public Citizen definition and emphasizing that it "narrowly cabins trade secrets to information relating to the 'productive process' itself").

[15] See, e.g., Herrick v. Garvey, 200 F. Supp. 2d 1321, 1326 (D. Wyo. 2000) ("'technical blueprints depicting the design, materials, components, dimensions and geometry of'" 1935 aircraft (quoting agency declaration)), aff'd, 298 F.3d 1184, 1190 n.3 (10th Cir. 2002) (noting requester's concession at oral argument that blueprints remained commercially valuable); Sokolow v. FDA, No. 1:97-CV-252, slip op. at 7 (E.D. Tex. Feb. 19, 1998) (description of how drug is manufactured, including "analytical methods employed to assure quality and consistency" and "results of stability testing")

general information concerning a product's physical or performance characteristics or a product formula when release would not reveal the actual formula itself[16].

In conclusion, one appellate court in the United States has concluded that "where the submitter or owner of documents held by the government grants the government permission to loan or release those documents to the public, those documents are no longer 'secret' for purposes of [trade secret protection under] ..." and so must be released[17].

---

[16] See Ctr. for Auto Safety, 244 F.3d at 151 (airbag characteristics relating "only to the end product -- what features an airbag has and how it performs -- rather than to the production process"); Nw. Coalition for Alternatives to Pesticides v. Browner, 941 F. Supp. 197, 201-02 (D.D.C. 1996) ("common names and Chemical Abstract System . . . numbers of the inert ingredients" contained in pesticide formulas).

[17] Herrick, 298 F.3d at 1194 & n.10 (distinguishing the facts of the case before it, and upholding trade secret protection nonetheless, based upon the subsequent revocation of that permission and the requester's failure to challenge both whether such revocation could legally operate to "restore the secret nature of the documents" and, if so, whether such revocation could properly be made after the documents had been requested under the FOIA).

Exemption for National Security Matters

The Freedom of Information Act 2011 (FOIA) gives rights of public access to information held by public institution yet it is clear that public a institution can refuse a request on the grounds of national security.

Thus, the law is clear that information should be exempted from disclosure if the exemption is required for the purpose of safeguarding national security.

The FOIA gives an exemption from disclosing information where the exemption is needed for the purpose of safeguarding national security. This exemption is subject to a public interest test.

Although, there is no definition of "National security" in the law it is capable of a wide interpretation. The interests of national security are not limited directly to preventing military and terrorist attacks within Nigeria's boundary but include the safety of Nigerian citizens overseas, the protection of our democratic constitution, the effective operation of national security bodies, and co-operation with other countries in fighting international terrorism.

When the FOIA was passing through UK Parliament, the House of Lords made it clear that the government should have significant discretion in determining what is in the interests of national security.

In the case of <u>Norman Baker MP v IC and Cabinet Office (EA/2006/0045; 28 February 2007)</u> the Information Tribunal held that the Cabinet Office was not required to release information about the Wilson doctrine, which covers the interception of MPs' telephones.

The tribunal decided it helpful to refer to a decision by the House of Lords (HL): <u>Secretary of State for the Home Department v Rehman ([2001] UKHL 47;</u>

[2003] 1 AC 153). In that case, it was held by the Law Lords that the interests of national security were not limited to preventing specific threats to the UK alone but included the protection of democracy, international co-operation and other aspects of the government's counter-terrorism policy.

The exemption under the law for safeguarding national security does not apply simply because the information relates to national security and it must be applied in a blanket fashion. There must be evidence to support the assertion that disclosure of the information requested would pose a real and specific threat to national security. In the case of Metropolitan Police v IC (EA/2008/0078; 30 March 2009), the Metropolitan Police Service (MPS) refused to allow a researcher to view Special Branch records dating from 1888 to 1917. A clear analysis of the two cases presented reveals that the request for information for matters related to national security will normally be refused if the request is not carefully drafted. In the above case cited earlier, the Metropolitan Police Service (MPS) argued that some of the material referred to the use of informants and that any disclosure would prejudice the police's ability to recruit informants in the future. The Information Commissioner rejected this argument as MPS had "not provided any evidence to demonstrate …real and specific threats"(ICO decision notice FS50106800). MPS subsequently presented convincing evidence to the Information Tribunal demonstrating that the names of informants should be withheld, but accepted that the rest of the material did not pose any risk. Even where the exemption is required for the purposes of safeguarding national security, the public interest test must be applied.

FOIA Judicial Decisions outside Nigeria

Since the enactment of the Freedom of Information Act 2011, only few cases have been successful.

Though, there has been a lot of rhetoric about the type of information people should be requesting under the Freedom of Information Act the fact remains that until more cases have been tested in the court, nobody is clear how the judges would decide whether specific public records should be disclosure or not.

However, there are precedents in other jurisdictions around the world that could help Nigerian judges in the better understanding of the application of the Act and this book provides a sample of decided cases and how the courts have arrived at their decisions. This is only a guide to assist Nigerian judges and barristers alike in their search for a better understanding of the FOI law.

An analysis of Code decisions between 1994 and 2002 by Meredith Cook (2003) reveals that the Ombudsman considered the public interest in 21 out of 106 decisions. Some of the 21 cases are summarised below.

Decisions where the public interest outweighed the harm likely to arise from disclosure

Case No A.1/97 Refusal to disclose information about the funding for a project to create a wetland habitat for birds

An interest group asked the Cardiff Bay Development Corporation for current cost estimates for the proposed wetland habitat. The Corporation refused to give a detailed breakdown of the overall £5.7 million budget citing exemption 7(a) (prejudice to competitive position of a public body) and exemption 10 (prematurity in relation to a planned publication). The Ombudsman accepted that disclosing estimates based on tender information might cause limited prejudice to the Corporation's position.

However, he held that the public interest in having up-to-date information about cost estimates outweighed any prejudice likely to arise from disclosure and that the estimates should be disclosed.

Case No A.31/00 Refusal to release internal advice about the closure of a fire station

The applicant asked the United Kingdom Home Office for reports about the proposed closure of a fire station. It refused to release the information citing exemption 2 (internal discussion and advice). The Ombudsman considered that exemption 2 applied to the decisions taken by Ministers in respect of the fire station. In assessing the public interest he said:

"That, in any given case, is clearly a matter of judgement. There is no doubt that there is a public interest in the complainant and the local interest group having sufficient information in order to represent effectively local interests in the issue. This would seem to point towards disclosure. But, this is still very much a live issue. There are also within the reports comments made on matters relating to the provision of fire services within the area which range rather wider than the specific issues of this station. On that basis I do not think it appropriate for me to recommend the complete disclosure of information but I do think it possible to disclose some of it without undermining the effectiveness of the Home Office's internal considerative processes."

Case No A. 26/01 Refusal to provide copies of correspondence between the Foreign and Commonwealth Office (FCO) and the Department of Trade and Industry (DTI) relating to human rights issues and the Ilisu Dam

During the Ilisu Dam project there were a number of exchanges between the Minister for Europe and the Chair of the House of Commons Select Committee on International Development concerning human rights issues and the Ilisu Dam project in Turkey. The Chair asked the Minister to provide him with copies of all relevant correspondence between the FCO and the DTI. The Minister refused citing exemption 2 (internal discussion and advice). The Ombudsman agreed that exemption 2 applied and was sympathetic to the government's view that releasing correspondence between departments on such a sensitive issue might well affect the candour with which those debating similar issues in the future feel they can record their views.

However he considered there were substantial counter arguments. There is a valid public interest in obtaining a clear answer to the question of the impact on human rights. The government itself had already recognised public interest in the project by placing its general assessments and judgements on the public record and therefore the public interest over rode the harm.

Case 98049—Information about successful tenders

The requester asked the Office for Public Works for all the documentation relating to a tender for army vehicles. Following consultation with the tenders under section 29, the Office of Public Works decided to release the Order Form relevant to each of the four parts of the tender, containing the successful tender's name, the tender price and the number and type of vehicle involved.

Three of the four successful tenders applied for a review of this decision by the Commissioner. They argued that section 26(1)(a) applied because the prices were given in confidence, on the understanding that they would be treated as confidential and that disclosure would be likely to prejudice the giving of similar information in the future. It was also argued that disclosure would constitute a breach of a duty of confidence within the meaning of section 26(1)(b). It was also claimed that the tender prices were commercially sensitive information within the meaning of section 27(1) and that the public interest did not require disclosure.

The Commissioner held that the public interest in openness and accountability resulting from disclosing tender prices outweighed any public interest in preventing commercial harm to the tenders and the tender process.

Case 98058—Information about the legislative process

The requester asked the Ministry of Justice for papers relating to the drafting of the Solicitors Amendment Bill 1998. The records at issue consisted of correspondence between the MOJ and the Law Society, records created by the Office of the Attorney General, a memorandum to the Government and earlier drafts, the Government decision about the Bill and copies of two published articles.

In relation to the information for which the Ministry could legitimately claim an exemption under section 26(1)(a) for information given in confidence, the Commissioner considered that on balance the information should be released in the public interest. He expressed the clear view that

"it is in the public interest that views and representations which influence the legislative process should be open to public scrutiny" and noted:

"Before the enactment of the Freedom of Information Act, significant weight might not have been attached to this aspect of the public interest. Indeed, it might have been assumed generally that the public interest was better served by conducting deliberations which preceded legislation on a confidential basis. However, the very enactment of the Freedom of Information Act suggests that significant weight should be attached to the public interest in an open and transparent process of government."

Case 98114 —Invoices paid by government departments to telecommunications companies

The requester sought access to copies of invoices paid to telecommunications companies by the Department of Finance. The Department decided to release all the records sought by the applicant. One of the telecommunication companies applied for a review of this decision under sections 27(1)(b) and 27(1)(c) of the Irish FoI Act. It argued that releasing the information could prejudice its ability to compete for future business from public bodies and that in the case of some products; it could also prejudice its ability to provide such products to customers who are not public bodies.

The Information Commissioner considered that the public interest in public bodies obtaining value for money and in openness about the expenditure of public funds was not absolute. However, he said that in this case, there was a significant public interest in ensuring that the public bodies concerned obtain value for money in purchasing telecommunication services and that this outweighed any public interest in protecting the telecommunications companies' commercial interests.

Case 98078—Records relating to the expenditure of health boards and voluntary hospitals

The requester asked the Department of Health and Children for various records relating to expenditure of health boards and voluntary hospitals. The Department refused access to the records and argued in its submission to the Commissioner that the records were exempt under sections 20(1)(a) and (b), 21(1)(b) and (c), 23(1)(a)(ii), 26, 27(1), 28 and 31.

The Commissioner considered the section 20 public interest test which provides that deliberations of public bodies may only be withheld if it would be contrary to the public interest to release the information. The Commissioner's comments are worth quoting in full because they illustrate that the test in section 20 establishes a high threshold which therefore makes it difficult to justify withholding information.

"The Department has taken a narrow view of the public interest. In the field of health care there are a number of issues to be considered in relation to the

public interest…the public interest is not limited to matters of cost efficiency alone. Where cutbacks of major importance to the provision of healthcare services are being made, there is also a public interest in the community knowing what these may be. The Department and the health agencies are administering the health services on behalf of the community. There is a public interest in the community knowing as much about how the services are being administered as is consistent with the provision of an efficient and effective service. This does not mean that the public has the right to know every proposal that is made. Indeed, there is a strong argument in favour of protecting proposals from release at an early stage in order to allow the public body to properly consider the matter. However, once the decision to proceed with any proposed action is taken, the need to withhold the release of the information weakens. Furthermore the argument advanced that the information once released will be used (or abused) in some particular way or misinterpreted or will not be properly understood reflects an attitude more akin to that which prevailed in an era dominated by the Official Secrets Act rather than one governed by the FoI Act."

Case 99168—Details of members' expenses

The requester sought access to the total expenses paid to each member of the Houses of the Parliament in relation to travel expenses, telephone and postage expenses, secretarial and office administration expenses and all other expenses paid since April 1998. The Houses argued that the personal information should be withheld.

The Commissioner held that that the public interest in ensuring accountability for the use of public funds greatly outweighed any right to privacy which the members might enjoy in relation to details of their expenses claims.

A whistleblower

An employee of Public Works and Government Services, Canada blew the whistle on contracting irregularities and misappropriation of government funds. There was an internal investigation and the employee subsequently asked for all of the papers. The department refused because it wanted to protect the privacy of the wrongdoers, who could be identified even if their names were omitted.

The Commissioner considered that there was a public interest in exposing instances of misappropriation of public funds and that this clearly outweighed any invasion of privacy. He was guided by comments made by Justice Muldoon of the Federal Court in the case of Bland v Canada (National Capital Commission):

"It is always in the public interest to dispel rumours of corruption or just plain mismanagement of the taxpayers' money and property. Naturally if there

has been negligence, somnolence or wrongdoing in the conduct of a government institution's operations it is by virtual definition, in the public interest to disclose it and not to cover it up in wraps of secrecy."

The Commissioner also noted that as a general rule before a department suppresses information about employee wrongdoing, even to protect privacy, the relative balance between the public interest in disclosure and privacy should be considered by the department's most senior officials.

Reneging on a promise

A journalist complained to the Commissioner because the Transportation Safety Board had refused to release air traffic control tapes and transcripts relating to a plane crash. The Commissioner considered that TSB did not properly consider the public interest override and that the public interest in air safety outweighed any privacy considerations.

Weighing public interest

A journalist requested the audit reports on 21 meatpacking companies from Agriculture Canada. Agriculture Canada consulted the companies and weighed the potential financial loss to competitive interests or interference with contract negotiations with the public interest in safeguarding public health. The complaint to the Commissioner was on a narrower unrelated issue, but the Commissioner noted that the:

"...only fair and reasonable way to balance public interest and corporate loss is do some measure of fact finding including facts from corporations."

Request for detailed information about Prime Minister's Office staff salaries Case No W4151769

A reporter requested details of staff salaries in the New Zealand PM's office from the Minister responsible for Ministerial services. The Minister refused on the grounds that it was necessary to protect privacy of the individuals concerned.

The Ombudsman agreed that releasing the detailed information would prejudice privacy, but considered that there was a public interest in the office expenditure given that the office was critical to the effectiveness of the PM in the discharge of her role. Following consultations with the Privacy Commissioner it was agreed that the Minister should release the total personnel expenditure and the number of staff involved and withhold details of each individual employee's salary.

Decisions where the public interest in disclosure did not outweigh the harm caused by disclosure

Case No A.5/94 Failure to supply to a third party information about a Department's discussions with industry representatives

The requester asked the Department of Health for information relating to discussions between the Department and pharmaceutical industry on a proposed code of practice. The Department withheld the information citing exemption 7 (non-disclosure of information prejudicial to effective management and operations of public service) and exemption 14 (information given in confidence). The Ombudsman held that no exemption applied to details of where, when and what was discussed, but accepted that the names of industry representatives involved could be withheld. Although there was a public interest in the substance of the discussions, there was no public interest in releasing the names of the specific identities involved.

Case No A.12/95 Unwillingness to release information relating to the repeal of the Northern Ireland broadcasting restrictions

The requester asked the Department of National Heritage to release papers generated in the course of a review of the broadcasting restrictions about interviewing members of certain organisations in Northern Ireland. The Department withheld the information citing exemption 2 (internal discussion and advice). The Ombudsman agreed that exemption 2 applied to internal documents only and in relation to those internal papers he did not consider that the public interest in disclosure overrode the potential harm to frankness and candour of future discussion. It was important that the issues considered sensitive were still topical and might arise again in the future for consideration.

Case No A.5/96 Refusal to disclose sale proceeds of certain British Rail businesses

The requester asked the Department of Transport to disclose the prices at which 27 British Rail businesses were sold to buyers in the private sector. The Department refused on the basis that disclosure of prices would prejudice future negotiations on the sale of British Rail's remaining assets although it was acknowledged that all the requested information would be made public at some stage. The Department cited exemption 7 (effective management and operations of the public service) and exemption 13 (third party commercial confidences). The Ombudsman agreed that in the circumstances the Department could withhold some of the prices under exemption 7 but not exemption 13, noting:

"It is common ground that the public interest requires the details of proceeds from the sale of assets formerly in public ownership should be made public. The question is: when? I appreciate the Department's argument that, where there remain to

be sold businesses akin to those already sold, the premature disclosure of the selling prices achieved is capable of having a prejudicial effect on the negotiations for the sale of the remaining businesses."

He considered that where releasing the price would not prejudice future negotiations (i.e. where there was no similarity between the business sold and businesses yet to be sold) the exemption did not apply.

Case No A.29/95 Refusal to provide information about the economic viability of the thermal oxide reprocessing plant (THORP) at Sellafield

The requester asked the Department of the Environment for a complex technical report by an external consultant about the economic viability of THORP. The Department refused citing exemption 13 (commercial confidentiality). The Ombudsman found that the public interest in making information about THORP available did not outweigh the interest in maintaining the exemption. It was significant that the technical report was consistent with the published public consultation paper and other than the fact it was more detailed, it did not make any further information available.

Case No A.15/96 Failure to disclose to a complainant an internal report into his complaint

The requester asked the Valuation Office Agency for an internal report into a complaint he had made to them about one of their district offices. The VOA refused citing exemption 2 (internal discussion and advice). The Ombudsman required the VOA to release purely factual information and in relation to the internal discussion, held that the public interest in making it available did not outweigh the potential harm to frankness and candour of internal discussion that might arise from disclosure.

Case No A.26/97 Refusal to disclose an internal report about matters raised in a complaint

A company was investigated by the Inland Revenue. The directors asked for the internal report made by the District Inspector concerning the investigation. The Inland Revenue refused citing exemption 2 (internal discussion and advice) and exemption 6 (effective management of the economy). The Ombudsman found that the public interest did not outweigh the harm that would result from disclosure. It was significant that the Inland Revenue had conducted the investigation in a "highly rancorous manner" and that there was a great degree of sensitivity on all sides. The directors already had the results of the investigation.

Case No A.13/97 Refusal to disclose information including telephone notes and internal legal advice from an individual's file

A family firm was in dispute with the Court Service about a default judgment entered in error against it. It asked to see all documents held by the Court Service about the case. The Court Service cited the legal privilege exemption. The Ombudsman held that exemption 2 (harm to frankness and candour of internal discussion) applied. He held that the public interest in making the information available did not outweigh the interest in maintaining the exemption.

Case No A.27/97 Refusal to disclose a report by a Board of Visitors

The applicant prisoner asked to see a copy of the prison Board of Visitors' annual report. The Northern Ireland Prison Service refused citing exemption 4(e) (law enforcement and legal proceedings) and exemption 7(b) (effective management and operations of the public service). Given the security situation in Northern Ireland, the Ombudsman agreed that the risk of harm if the reports were disclosed outweighed the public interest in making information available.

Case No A.23/99 Refusal to release information relating to the development of encryption policy

The director of an organisation concerned with the interaction between information technology and society, asked the Department of Trade and Industry for information relating to the formulation of the government's policy on encryption. In particular he asked for names of officials on the Cryptographic Policy Working Group (CPWG). The DTI refused to release policy advice citing exemptions 1 (defence, security and international relations), 2 (internal discussion and advice) and 4 (law enforcement and legal proceedings). The Ombudsman considered the public interest in releasing names of officials and held that:

"In general I consider that the balance of the public interest will normally favour disclosure of

information regarding which organisations are represented on a body such as the CPWG; it is also likely to be reasonable to indicate the seniority *of the representatives. However, it is less likely to be in the public interest to disclose the names of individual members if they are members of such bodies as representatives of their organisations: any suggestion for example that they should be held personally answerable for the views which they had expressed would clearly be misplaced. I am not persuaded that releasing the identities of those attending the meetings is required in the public interest."[original author's emphasis]*

Case No A.2/00 Refusal to release copies of four internal performance reports

The applicant asked the Ministry of Defence for four internal MOD reports relating to departmental performance. The MOD refused citing exemption 1 (defence, security and international relations) and exemption 2 (internal discussion and advice). In relation to information concerning nuclear capability and security and intelligence matters the Ombudsman held that the possible harm caused by release was **not** outweighed by the "considerable public interest that might justify making that information more widely known."

Case No A. 2/01 Refusal to release information about a London Transport project

The applicant asked for the data that was available to the Department of Environment, Transport and the Regions Ministers when making their decision to award the Prestige contract to an international consortium of companies known as TranSys. In particular the applicant requested the data that had been used in the evaluation that is known as the public sector comparator. DETR refused, citing exemptions 2, 7, 14 and also exemption 13 (harm to competitive position of third party). The Ombudsman held that exemption 13 had been correctly cited and that although there was a strong public interest in matters relating to public transport in London, it did not outweigh the potential harm that could be.

Nigerian FOIA Judicial Decisions

Since the enactment of the Freedom of Information Act 2011 some landmark decisions had been made by judges in Nigeria and below are some of the cases:

BONIFACE OKEZIE V. ATTORNEY-GENERAL OF THE FEDERATION AND THE ECONOMIC AND FINANCIAL CRIMES COMMISSION

Court Decision Summarised - Public institutions must comply with requests for information within seven days. If they refuse to comply, they must supply specific basis for refusal under the FOI Act in a notice to the applicant within seven days of the request.

Facts of the case -

On 26 January 2012, Boniface Okezie requested from the Attorney-General of the Federation the following pieces of information relating to the operations of the Ministry of Justice: 1) a list of criminal prosecutions being carried out through private lawyers; 2) the total amount spent in the course of the said prosecutions and the source of funding; 3) the amount the Ministry of Justice pays to its legal officers; 4) the amount the Ministry of Justice spent in training its legal officers over the past year; and 5) the reason for abandoning the legal officers in the Ministry of Justice in favor of private lawyers. On the same day, Okezie also requested similar items of information from the Economic and Financial Crimes Commission (EFCC), in addition to information regarding the EFCC's monetary dealings with Cecilia Ibru, the former Managing director of Oceanic Bank.

Both the Ministry of Justice and the EFCC acknowledged receipt of the requests for information but failed to comply with the requests. When Okezie brought a suit against the Attorney-General and the EFCC to compel disclosure, the Attorney-General denied that the government had deliberately refused Okezie's request, instead claiming that "the request by the Plaintiff [was] being processed, and due to the classified nature of the request, the Ministry need[ed] to collate the data relating to financial issues from the Finance Department and the other department handling training matters."The EFCC argued that the Federal High Court in Lagos "lacked territorial jurisdiction," since "the cause of action arose in Abuja, and . . . the head office of the EFCC was in Abuja."The EFCC also advanced that "the Plaintiff had no locus standi to institute [the] action, that the nature of the information would infringe on state security and the right of the lawyers in relation to client and solicitor relationship."

Decision

At the outset, the Court established that the "basic principle behind most freedom of information legislation is that the burden of proof falls on the body asked for information, not on the person asking for it."

As such, the individual requesting information "does not usually have to give an explanation for their actions, but if the information is not disclosed a valid reason has to be given." To comport with individuals' rights to request information under the FOI Act, public institutions are expected to convey the requested information "promptly but not later than seven days after it has received a request." Where a request is denied, the institution must "give notice to the Applicant" stating the basis for refusal within the FOI Act "within seven days." Since the Attorney-General did not appear to be "contesting the case on the merits" and provided no basis under the Act for not supplying the information, the Court concluded that the Attorney-

General "ha[d] no . . . power under the law" to have "kept mute."

The Court also rejected in large part the various arguments advanced by the EFCC. Mainly, the EFCC erred in claiming that the Court lacked territorial jurisdiction because the action was not brought in Abuja. It found that such rules of civil procedure are "not mandatory, but directory."Moreover, even if the EFCC's headquarters were in Abuja, it was a "known fact that the [EFCC] carries on [a] substantial part of its business . . . in Lagos."

As to the locus standi issue, the Court held that it is not necessary for a plaintiff "to demonstrate any specific interest in the information being applied for" to have standing to bring suit. Rather, the requester of information was "entitled as a Citizen of [Nigeria] to institute [the] proceeding to compel the Defendants . . . to comply with the provisions of the Freedom of Information Act."

As to the other two exceptions raised by the EFCC, the Court noted that while the EFCC was "entitled to protect information that is properly classified in the interest of national security," and while "some of the information requested [...] threatened national security", the EFCC still had the duty to respond to the request. With respect to EFCC's attorney-client privilege argument, the Court acknowledged that such an exemption did exist (see Section 14(1)(a) of the FOI Act) but explained that it was not able to opine on the issue. "Whether there exists a confidentiality agreement" is "an issue of fact," and the EFCC failed to provide specific information on the "nature of the relationship."

Finally, the Court addressed the issue of fees paid by the defendants to their legal practitioners by referring to an earlier judgment finding that such information would "interfere with the contractual or other negotiations of a third party", and that public interest in disclosure, in this case, does not outweigh the protected interest.

INCORPORATED TRUSTEES OF THE CITIZENS ASSISTANCE CENTRE V. HONOURABLE S. ADEYEMI IKUFORIJI & LAGOS STATE HOUSE OF ASSEMBLY

Court Decision Summarised - The Freedom of Information Act 2011 cannot be applied retroactively to requests for information that originated prior to the enactment of the Act. An order of mandamus is an extraordinary remedy that should only be granted when all other judicial remedies have been exhausted.

Facts of the case -

On July 14, 2011, the Incorporated Trustees of the Citizens Assistance Centre (Incorporated Trustees) requested information regarding government overhead costs from 1999 to September 2011. When the Lagos State House of Assembly, the state legislature, did not comply with the request, the Incorporated Trustees requested from the Court an order of mandamus compelling disclosure of the information. The Lagos State House of Assembly supplied several counter-arguments: 1) the Incorporated Trustees lacked locus standi to bring suit as they were not a registered organization and "not a juristic person"; 2) "the overhead costs sought to be published cannot be published without creating crisis in the interest of the state and its security"; 3) disclosure would cause government employees to "suffer irreparable injury and/or prejudice" and the information was thus subject to the personal information exemption in Section 14 of the FOI Act; and 4) the FOI Act could not be applied retroactively as it took effect on 28 May 2011 after the period that the requested information concerns.

Decision

The Court first dispensed with the argument that the Incorporated Trustees lacked locus standi to bring suit: "it is trite law that only juristic persons can sue or be sued." Rather, "juristic persons" takes on a broad meaning and includes "natural persons, incorporated companies, corporations with perpetual succession and unincorporated associations granted the status of legal persons by law."

However, the FOI Act could not be applied retroactively. The preamble to the Act "answers the [retroactivity] question succinctly," as the preamble makes no mention of retroactivity. It would have "clearly stated" so had the Act been intended to apply retroactively. In the absence of a clear intention within the text, "an interpretation giving retrospective effect to a statute should not be readily accepted where that would affect vested rights or impose liability or disqualification for past events."

The Court also considered the fact that the Incorporated Trustees "delayed beyond the 30 days approved by section 20 of the Act before filing the action." Given the "extraordinary and residuary remedy" of an order of mandamus, the Incorporated Trustees' failure to comply with the procedural guidelines was "fatal to their application "for information.

The Court has the power to refuse an order of mandamus at its discretion and "will not grant the order if a specific alternative remedy which is equally convenient, beneficial and effectual is available."

Lastly, the Court agreed with the State House of Assembly that the personal information contained within the requested information rendered it subject to the exception in Section 14 of the Act since public interest in disclosure, in this case, did not outweigh the protection of privacy. Specifically, the requested information fell under Section 14(1), which provides that a public institution "must deny an application for information that contains personal information and information exempted under the section which includes personnel files and personal information maintained with respect to employees, appointees or elected officials of any public institution or applicants for such positions."

LEGAL DEFENCE & ASSISTANCE PROJECT (GTE) LTD. V. CLERK OF THE NATIONAL ASSEMBLY OF NIGERIA

Court Decision Summarised - The salaries of the Members of Parliament are not personal information and should be disclosed.

Facts of the case -

The Legal Defence & Assistance Project (LEDAP) is a registered non-governmental organization that aims to promote "good governance, public accountability, and the rule of law in Nigeria"(p. 4).

On 6 July 2011, LEDAP applied to the National Assembly of Nigeria (NAN) for information "on details of salaries, emolument, and allowances paid to the Honourable Members of Representatives and Distinguished Senators, both of the 6th Assembly, from June 2007 to May 2011"(p. 4). The Assembly did not respond to the request, prompting LEDAP to bring a suit in the High Court (p. 4).

The NAN argued primarily that the applicant did not file within the time limit set in Section 20 of the FOI Act, that it would be "prejudicial "to pending cases to grant LEDAP's request; and that the information constituted personal information that was exempted under Section 14 of the Act. (p. 5).

Decision

The Court denied the argument regarding late filing, agreeing with LEDAP that Section 20 of the Act granted the Court discretion to extend the time limitations for filing suit (p. 8).

Before looking into the exceptions, the Court emphasized that "the onus . . . is on the denying authority to show that it is justified by the Act to deny the information requested"(p. 19). With respect to the "prejudicial" argument, the Court found that the NANs explanation for "what interest . . . will be prejudiced" had to do with a jurisdictional issue that was irrelevant to the present proceedings (p. 21). Since the Court could not "speculate" as to the actual relevance, the NAN's rationale was "not justified by the Act"(p. 21). Nor was the NAN's Section 14 argument persuasive. After reviewing the wording of the relevant provision, the Court concluded that LEDAP "did not request any of the personal information relating to the Honourable Members, but simply what was paid to them while they were in service from the public fund," and that such information was "not among those exempted" under Section 14(1) of the Act (p. 24).

Public & Private Development Centre v. Power Holding Company of Nigeria & the Honorable Attorney-General of the Federation

Court Decision Summarised - Disclosure of information about an already-awarded contract — one that is no longer in the stages of negotiations —does not interfere with the rights of the third party contractor.

Facts of the case -

On 30 August 2012 the Public & Private Development Centre Ltd. (PPDC) requested information from the Power Holding Company of Nigeria regarding the award of a contract for the supply and installation of 300 power units in several Nigerian cities (p. 5). Among the requested items were a procurement plan for the project, the bidding documents issued to all interested bidders on the project, a list of all contractors that submitted bids, a copy of the bid evaluation, the minutes of the board meeting where the winning bids were approved, and copies of final contract award documents (p. 2-3). The Power Holding Company of Nigeria and the Attorney-General of the Federation refused to furnish the requested information, prompting the PPDC to bring suit (p. 5).

Decision

The main issue before the Court was the Power Holding Company of Nigeria's argument that the requested information fell under Section 15(1)(b) of the Act (p. 6), which allows public institutions to "deny an application for information that contains information the disclosure of which could reasonably be expected to interfere with the contractual or other negotiations of a third party"(p. 7). Since the bid evaluation report involved contractual information between the Power Holding Company and the third party company who won the contract, Crown Resources Development Co. Ltd., the Power Holding Company claimed it to be an injustice to the third party contractor and a breach of the privity of contract doctrine to grant PPDC's request for information (p. 7-8).

Considering the Section 15(1)(b) argument, the Court first outlined that a scrutiny of the provision indicates that three conditions must be concurrently present for a public institution to deny a request for information on these grounds:
(1) the transaction must still be at the negotiation stage,
(2) a third party must be involved, and
(3) the disclosure of the information must reasonably be expected to interfere with the contractual or other negotiations of a third party (p. 8).

The Court found that the first condition had not been met. Rather, "the uncontroverted Evidence before the Court state[d] unequivocally [that] the negotiations [had been] concluded" well before PPDC had made its request (p. 8).

Moreover, even if the transaction had been at the negotiation stage at the time of PPDC's request, the third condition also would not have been met.

According to the Court, "the disclosure of the information sought by [PPDC] cannot by any stretch of the imagination reasonably be expected to interfere with any contractual or other negotiations of the . . .third party"(p. 9).

Absent these two conditions necessary for Section 15(1)(b) to apply, the Court ordered the Power Holding Company of Nigeria to produce the requested information.

UZOEGWU F.O.C. ESQ V. CENTRAL BANK OF NIGERIA & ATTORNEY-GENERAL OF THE FEDERATION

Facts of the case -

In November 2011 Uzoegwu requested from the Central Bank of Nigeria (CBN) information regarding "the amount payable to the Governor, Deputy Governor and Directors of the CBN as monthly salary"(p. 2-3). The CBN did not reply, although the Director of Finance at the CBN had acknowledged receipt of the request (p. 3). One month later, Uzoegwu filed an Originating Summons in the High Court, to which the CBN and the Attorney-General of the Federation responded by arguing that the requested information was "personal information which was communicated to [the officers] upon their appointments" at the CBN"(p. 3). The CBN also argued that "the information is protected by trade and commercial secrets (section 15(1)) read together with section 13(3) (training of officials) of the Act"(p. 4-5).

Decision

First, the Court examined the Central Bank's claim that the information was "protected by Section 15(1) read together with Section 13(3)"of the Act and found the argument to be muddled. For one thing, Section 13 of the Act does not have any subsections and is in no sense related to trade and commercial secrets (p. 8-9). As for Section 15(1), the Court concluded that "the salaries of the Governor of the CBN and Deputy Governors and Directors of the Bank cannot, by any stretch of imagination, be trade secrets contemplated by . . . Section 15(1)"(p. 10).

However, the central question before the Court was whether the requested information regarding the salaries of high-level officials of the CBN qualified as "personal information" under Section 14(1) of the Act. Section 14(1) provides that a public institution "must deny" a request for information "that contains personal information," which "includes" several types of personal information listed, none of which pertain to salaries of public officials (p. 13). While the CBN argued that the word "include" indicated a non-exhaustive list, the Court was not convinced, "for the simple reason that the salaries and allowances of officers are such intrinsic part of their public employment or appointment that if the legislature intended to exempt them as personal information[...], they will have stated so clearly"(p. 14).

In fact, the Court claimed it would "not [be] logical to say that the payments of public officers from the public funds for their services to the public is personal information"(p. 15). Moreover, the Court claimed that the remaining subsections of Section 14 indicate that "where the interest of the public is in clash with the individual interest . . . the collective interest must be held paramount"(p. 16). Namely, the Court relied on Sections 14(2) and 14(3), which provide certain situations where even information that is protected as personal information under Section 14(1) may be disclosed (p. 15-16). By the wording of Section 14(3) of the Act, the "legislature clearly intended that the public interest [be] placed above all else, including the personal interest of the individuals"(p. 17). As such, the Court ordered disclosure of the information about the salaries of CBN officials.

FOIA Compliance – Public Institution Checklist

Since the signing into law by Nigeria former President, Dr Goodluck Ebele Jonathan, of the Freedom of Information Act, there has been very little progress across the 36 states of the federation on the adoption and readiness to ensure that requesters (submitters) of information get access to public record.

In the first six months of the introduction of the Freedom of Information Act, only Lagos State and Ekiti State had adopted the Act locally and ensured some form of accessibility to government records.

However, the Freedom of Information Act 2011 sets out clearly what public institutions are expected to do in readiness for the compliance with the Act and below area checklist of things that public institutions should do to ensure conformity with FOIA:

1. Public institutions should identify records that they hold and ensure that they are in a format that requesters (submitters) are able access. The Freedom of Information Act requires public institutions to comply with a list of documents and that is covered under section 3 of the FOIA 2011

2. Public institutions are expected to respond back to the request for information within 7 days of receiving it

3. Public institutions are expected to train all key staff in the usage and application of the Freedom of Information Act 2011

4. Public institutions must appoint a designated person to be responsible for responding to FOI requests on behalf of the public authority

5. A Public institution's website should have a record about how to request for information, type of information kept by the organization and previous requests that have been released to the public

If a public institution ensures that proper record management system principles are adhered to and staff are trained on the application of the FOI Act then it would easily educate the citizenry about their right to information and accessibility of it.

Appendix

Frequently asked questions

1. What is the Freedom of Information Act about?

The Freedom of Information Act (FOI Act) is a the Law that gives anyone a right of access to records, documents and information held by the

Government or government institutions and agencies as well as private bodies performing public functions, subject to certain exemptions.

2. What new rights will the Act give me as a Nigerian?

It will give every Nigerian the right to apply for information and records held by Government or government institutions and agencies within 7 days.

3. Do I have to give reasons why I want information?

Section 2(2) of the Act specifically provides that an applicant does not need to demonstrate any specific interest in the information he or she is applying for, which means that he or she does not need to explain why the information is being requested.

4. How do I make the request for information?

An applicant is expected under Section 4 of the Act to apply for access to a record or document in writing and to provide sufficient detail in the application to enable a member of staff of the public institution, with a reasonable effort, to identify the record.

5. Can I make an oral or informal request for information?

Yes. The FOI Act makes provision fora blind or illiterate applicant to make an oral request and for the designated public institution contact to transcript the information in order to respond to the request.

6. How do I know if the information I require exists and who has custody of it?

Section 3 of the FOI Act compels every government institution, department or agency, through its head, to publish a description of its responsibilities, the records under its control, administrative manuals, etc.

This is intended to give members of the public information about the records and information available in these institutions so that they know where to apply for the records or documents they are interested in.

7. From which government institution or private body can I apply for information?

Any citizen can apply for records and information from any government ministry, department, agency parastatal, etc., at any tier of government, whether Federal, State, or Local Government. Applications for records or information can also be made to private bodies or companies that are performing public functions.

8. What sort of information can I apply for?

A Nigerian citizen can apply for any record or information in the custody of any government institution, department or agency, as well as private bodies or companies performing public functions, subject to those categories of records and documents that are exempted from general public access.

9. Can I be denied access to any record or information?

Yes, if it falls within the categories of materials exempted under the FOI Act.

10. When I apply, how do I know if I will be given access or if access is denied?

Section 5 of the FOI Act requires the head of the government institution to which a requester submits a request for information to provide the information in writing within 7 days. However, it is worth mentioning that in the adopted version signed into law in both Lagos and Ekiti States, the applicant is expected to receive information within 14 working days of submitting the request.

11. If I am denied access to information, how can I seek redress?

You can seek legal redress by submitting an application for judicial review at the court. The FOI Act allows for the applicant to make an application within 30 days after he or she has been informed that access will not be given or when access is deemed to have been refused because no response was received within 7 days.

The court may, where necessary, extend this time limit. An application to the court shall be heard and decided summarily so as prevent delays.

12. Will I have to pay for information if I am granted access?

Yes, but the fees are limited to reasonable standard charges for search, duplication and transcription.

13. Can I apply for personal information held by the government?

Personal information is exempted from the general right of access. This includes: files and personal information about clients; patients; residents; students; or other individuals receiving social, medical, educational, vocational, financial, supervisory or custodial care or services directly or indirectly from federal agencies, government or public institutions.

14. What happens if the information I need has been altered or deleted from the records?

Any alteration to information under the Freedom of Information Act 2011 is deemed to be a criminal offence under section 10 of the Act and punishable by one year imprisonment on conviction for this offence.

15. If I have a disability can I get a record in a special format, like Braille?

The FOI Act provides that record and information should be given to the applicant in the format that he or she wants it, either in audio, visual, or transcribed formats.

Help on FOIA Application & Implementation

Nigerian Freedom of Information Act 2011 requires the training of staff on the application of the law. Non-compliance with a request within the time allowed could attract a huge fine after a judicial review application.

 This is a unique opportunity to avoid the embarrassment, fine and even criminal offence committed by your staff due to lack of understanding of the FOI law.

I can assist you with:

- designing and development of an FOI Strategy for your organisation

- Training of your senior management on FOI

- Training of your junior staff on application, monitoring and evaluation of FOI

About The Author

Temitope Olodo is an expert in PreventiveTerrorism, Information Practitioner and a Security Strategist based in the United Kingdom. One of Africa's foremost diaspora security and FOI expert in Europe. Temi published his first FOI book in 2012 entitled: **"Freedom of Information: A Practical Guide For Nigerians"**

He worked for Her Majesty's Government in many sensitive, strategic roles and departments including the Office for Criminal Justice Reform (OCJR), former Office of the Deputy Prime Minister (ODPM) and secondment to the Metropolitan Police etc. His first FOI job was over a decade ago and he was trained in UK Civil Service on FOI implementation and management.

Temi is a regular guest on radio and TV stations. He is the recipient of GAB's award on Security.

About The Book

Nigeria Former President, Goodluck Ebele Jonathan GCFR, gave his assent to Nigeria Freedom of Information Bill ending a long tortuous journey that started on 9th of December 1999 when it was first gazetted.

President Muhammad Buhari GCFR promised to confront the FOI challenges and said: "I pledge to... encourage proactive disclosure of information by government institutions in the spirit of the Freedom of Information Act..."

The author in this book sheds more light on the challenges associated with the implementation of the Freedom of Information Act and how to overcome the hurdles...

www.ingramcontent.com/pod-product-compliance
Lightning Source LLC
Chambersburg PA
CBHW072222170526
45158CB00002BA/714